Living... & Pure Poetry

Volume 1

Written & Illustrated by: Jamie Cowling

Dedication ————————————————————

I dedicate this book to those who choose to chase their dreams. To those who choose to love the beauties and tragedies of living.

To the artists: may you always be able to create- for the world would not be the same without us given the space to express our gifts.

To the children of this Earth: may you grow and seek light in all that you do. This Earth is a gift- just as each life is a gift. May you seek to cherish it with compassion, truth, and spirit.

To everyone I love and anyone I am yet to love: I thank you all for being the beautiful people that you are. Who we choose to be in this life- or the many – has so many effects upon a multitude of measures.

My family, my kin, blood related or otherwise- so much love to you! I would not be who I am without your support, instilled determination, and tough love. The kind that only we know and share dually fills me with gratitude.

This is my gift to all of you, may the lives that this book comes into or across be a connection for you... a connection to positivity, joy, truth, and love.

May the words of these pages find you when they are supposed too!

May they find you well

Introduction...

She awoke her sleepy eyes from their dreams...creating manifesting--- souls inspiring

Following the tunes frequency – interlocked – released- transposed- attained---loved—let go of... when understood

The light beams resonated universes upon universes

Stemming formulations – existence –resistance- knowing- seeking- finding---teaching - healing

How every ounce of its blue light came from the waters ripples

Lived- living –in----dove in – rode in- flowed in- was forged in

She pays attention to people, to galaxies, to energy

Shifting mind states – how simple the sweet nectars peaks acceptance

Evolutionary strains – cellular memory and navigation.

Creating vibrations within its gaining based upon roots grounded

Minds elevated

Energy experienced ----every portion of joy encompassing the worst of pains

Noticing

Fractals portions- synching what always felt like has been missing.

She wakes up – taps into

Vocal strings---- her songs sung – shedding spiritual pulses

Able to release it all once

More the vessels feeling it all – careful and thoughtful the motions—live and understand and love humanity.

Truth exists not in escaping

The melody of your very own journey ---some call it the calling of one's soul

I call it living and pure poetry – truth mediums placed in sectors crossings.

Table of Contents

Imagination.. 7

Lotus Blossoms.. 9

Oceanic Paradise.. 12

Energy... 15

Forever Live the Dream.. 21

Too Soon to Say Goodbye... 24

Travel... 28

Time to Shift to the Stars... 29

Star Crossed for Eternity.. 33

Colors of the Ocean.. 36

Replacing Nothing...Remembering Everything............... 40

Fairy Tale Drops on Pages Unseen.............................. 46

Sanctuary... 47

Encompassing Enchantment.. 49

Time Travelers Ways.. 51

Doorways...dots and places 54

At a Glance it became a Story..................................... 57

No Mind.. 59

A little sum, then sum thing... 62

Imprints of a Stone.. 69

Connectivity.. 77

Blessed by a Child... 79

Understanding...82

Moon Beams...84

Music...86

Nightly Love...88

Butterflies Guiding Grace...90

Blue Skies...93

Technology Plague...96

Circumstances of Living...98

A Trembling World...104

Awakening the Ancients...107

Connective Love...110

Dawn of Life...112

Can We Give...115

What it was to Dream...118

Transmigration...121

Surfing and Falling in Love...125

Paths...127

Release...131

Protective Eyes...133

Sage...135

Adia...137

Money...139

Painted Love...141

Respecting Natures Purity.. 143

The Little Things.. 145

Hands.. 147

Start Walking.. 151

Questioning Oneself..157

11 Times of Beauty... 164

Faith... 166

Guides.. 173

Become What You Create.. 176

Orb Guides (peak into Living...& Pure Poetry, Vol. II)....................181

Interview with the Author.. 183

Imagination

It begins with a dream

A short coming of time

Imagining what your life may be like in the following years to come

A picture

A posted brief flash- of how things will end up

Or with whom you will spend the rest of your days

If growing old with that person even exists... it makes you wonder if the answers will ever come
~ or if all you've done really amounts to anything at all...

And within all of this waiting for the perfect days

WE FORGET TO DREAM OF NEW ONES;

We forget to dream of new dreams...we forget to dream about what it was to dream...

And the vastness of the oceans within our eyes seems to fade, until all that is left is the
blindness of ourselves

Left in the dusted doorways of our minds

And then you wake up

You begin to remember exactly who you are

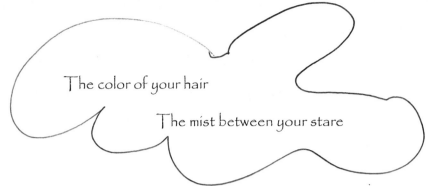

The color of your hair

The mist between your stare

And the very mystery that fills the cracks beneath your feet

They become real.............................

It is almost as familiar as the waking moments inside the dream

But it was your dream, with important substance and supreme quality.

You begin to move forward- you move on, and even if for a brief moment in time you begin to understand

That the dream is a distinct part of living: and that your life is the moment that is part of the dream.

It never ends

And it always begins

Imagination is its peak

And the remembrance of it

Is precisely what keeps it alive

Cross over now

Dimensions you feel

Understand exactly

How everything

Is connected

Lotus Blossoms

Lotus blossoms rise next to the rhythm of each step taken

Before the master of her time here – spent last laugh before

Light comes down to carry the burden of grace down off

Of her

   -   She steps-

Towards a world that is unknown

A part of her soul

Feelings shaken

For this place holds a space that

Cannot be seen

Only imagined

She finds it again

Holds the gate open and closes it when its time

Sometimes she may have to be reminded

That what lies ahead is real

For the truth resides close to the touch of what is created

And held

In front of the eyes of those who choose to see

The depths

Of the oceans

She contains inside...

Gliding smoothly

Now

Heading in a steady direction

Of

Unity

The visions reality unfolds itself upon her now

As she gives the sight back

Transfers its purity transfixed

Holding her palms out to the worlds

Watching them grow

Patiently

Knowing

Its essence lies

In becoming one with each direction

Divine inspiration formulates motion

Light beams of innocent energy

As she watches the children grow collectively

Smiles rain upon their faces

Running wild amongst the trees

Sustaining a connection

That runs oh so deep

Switching

In

To a

Simple   state   of   truly   living

Desire withstands about all it can take at times

And within the raging waters and fiery smokeless wind lies spirit

A calling off the main shore to come back again

To find green coated destinies with mountainous peaks of protruding everglade passion

Beside what is lost-

Lies something that is found

Beneath the crevasse of an old dirty shoe

Laces found along shoreline drops and sea shell crops in the middle of her sandy skirt

Left to battle the winds that convey her very soul

It is here where she rises like the suns pinks and blues

Here that the life begins to match the vortex

With a warm and delicate touch

Pure poetry truly

Its setting sails overlook tropical greens

A lime green, an almost yellowish green

Without questions of were to sail off to next, just follow the wind and you shall see, just follow the wind and life brings ease

No more suffering, no more pain, or confusion or doubt

Just complete understanding

Absolute meditating relief

As the wave breaks against her back

Riveting points convey deep ends

Pushing with all of what is left inside

Catching its bluish white peak

Fingertips glossing the inside of this circular symmetry

The swell of perfect aligned mastery

As her legs move back and forth and side to side

One now with the waters understanding, bending to its will, thankful

She rides it all the way home...

                                        Then, she jumps back in and starts to paddle again...

It is here that I belong

It is where my back is strong and my words have all of their meaning, it is here that makes the
most sense to me

The water is my palace and the sea puts all decisions at ease with the rhythm forever undying
– even unto the night

She still speaks without speaking

And see's without looking

It is here where I belong; the oceans sounds sung

Creating remedies

Becoming-living-feeling at one with

Everything

```Energy

Some days change doesn't always come in right,

Some day's its prevalent, evident, known – yet filled with uncertainty

Doesn't change how I still feel it

The vibrations still come through me;

Some days in my sleep-

Other times through visions,

And the frequency rises as the pulses keep rising, awareness transpires – as I tune into the relevance of the people-

My eyes open again- clearly

It is then that the healing notions flow within- to help all that I can –

Cellular mutations and truthful intentions- white pure light resonating resilience

We find a way...

As the frequency of equipping my soul with enough to not fold, then understand, minus the tsunamis' powerful entity...

It can feel tricky- but then it makes sense again- when it is supposed to – the gifts of this new way are the definition of harmony...

My body feels like a harnessing center- like a crystal in the earth – in the fire- cooled by the water- then reformed by the sky...

Pulses pass, then accumulate, then break free again – sent out via wave lengths once my body can no longer hold what is going on- I reset- resend – then reshape the negative- trying effortlessly to not drown in the process...

I move for the cause that is not of this place

I teach for the reasons beyond their own- I see things quickly and get annoyed by having to do everything their way...

It feels like I am being watched- but I don't care about what they see because- what I show is for their wisdom to develop-

Just as my vessels come from the vastness of the God(s) I know...

Help them see

Help them breath

Help them dream

Help them walk

Help them grow – and then explore why what is or was important – was never so...

New lives, new minds, new waves, new motions minus the limitation set forth by the ones that mean to control the rest

False pretense

   ...   Diminishes as emotions break context

   Converging vortex

      For it is here where I am from

————————Travel often

Laugh everyday

Love hard, and long and true

Smile at the moments that make memories

Lead with your heart- take care of your body

And even if they aren't ready

Learn to leap anyway

Find the depths of your soul

For the depths of your soul yearn for it

Create the sanctity of spaces unlike the rest...

Spaces exist in many forms

--------Where there is darkness

Light heals the un-rested

Close your eyes tonight knowing

That every little thing you do-

Every pull you are attracted to

Is for a reason

-Transcending you knowingly

Other times-

It may just be that push when the pull is too tight

Yet breath, knowing what embellishes each place rhythmically --- is beautiful

Make the music ...that photographs the sky

Paint the images passed on and on

By.............................and ....by... to another form of life---connecting almost by
exquisite accident

Choose to live in the light of your own truth-

Choose your own path- design your own landscape

Inspired by what so many miss out on seeing

Some souls grow too concerned with living

While all the while forgetting to truly live

Missing pieces

Leading unto fractions of your life

That should have been so much more

Empty....empty ... empty...they become---

When your cup is already filled up eternally

You see...simply choose to see

That no amount of palaces, possessions, stacks of golden treasures hold any value

-Especially not over true happiness

For love; a good meal, a comfortable place to stay-

-Where you can laugh and cry with the ones you love

See that - that is beautiful, and that feeling ---is the type of kind that can only be cherished

You see--------------------------

Humility resides in our humanity !

And that kind of love is within

All you ever needed was you-

And the recognition of how incredibly powerful free will designates, formulates

And paints -the dimensions of our own dreams...   Wow !

It is ever changing.................................

Yet

It is when we allow it to manifest

That we become rooted in the energy connected

We become observers to its beauty

We begin to see each form of life

How it grows

How it travels

How it survives gracefully,

Just as the seed that blossoms

Just as the child whose stare is attracted to empathy

Our sight then grows collectively

Pathways stream – it is all here – and always has been poetically justified

Can you see?

Will you choose to see...?

Forever Live the Dream

It is funny how sometimes you believe that in order for happiness

To be achieved you have to run away from everything that feels familiar

But in essence; happiness can be found with the peace of oneself inside the clarity of one's mind

And the energy of one's heart

All that is familiar to me is surrounded by the life that I create

Or have created so far

And rather than grieve what's ahead

One should enjoy it –look forward to it

Love and cherish every moment of it

Even if it's the most mundane piece of it all

I sometimes dream to be elsewhere

On an island

Always in that pool of green and blue skies that is filled with mystery and adventure

And there I go

Riding the wave of freedom

Once more

Once again–it's there

And I am happy again

And it's all just a memory without borders or limits

Costs me nothing

No amount of money in the world could occupy that dream

Nor ease... that sense-

That breath- no mind

Away from the silence within –without regret, or circumstance

Resistance ... or pride

I simply made the choice

And I was free

And all the long hard work it took to finally reach that moment has paid for itself

You can take the island from the girl

But you can never take the girl from the island – her sanctuary – her space

As little and miniscule as it may seem

Almost as if it doesn't exist at all

But it's there

A part of everything that matters and all that is true

The motion of her path ever swelling and sustaining a passage home

To the rhythm of her sound

Beating against the sands of time- a time that never needed existing

Because every moment was as good as it would ever desire to become

Even the hard ones fit into place just right as she began to choose...to

FOREVER LIVE HER DREAMS.

Too Soon to Say Goodbye...

It's a funny thing love is...

When we go through the motions

Delve deeply into the oceans of our pain

Look our losses in the mirror

Feel our hearts pounding in our chests, we realize so much

And when we feel as if we cannot go on- something steps in

Something so powerful that it brings you right back to the very start of what has the energy to heal almost anything

           Love

-and some of us are lucky enough

       -to find

     -those that we truly love in our lifetime

      -in this space

Some of us find and show love

     -to those we hold dear to our hearts

And some

      -Show love to anyone- regardless of memory or kinship...

Sometimes love and those we love are ripped from our grasp too soon – without ever giving us a chance to say goodbye

Or understand why...

Or even feel that love again in its physical form

       -In front of our eyes when we open them,

      -Upon our ears when we are but a phone call away,

    -Touched by the warmth of their hand in your own

And as we grieve through that which was lost -

    -We find that the love we have for one another holds us

       Like the crazy glue

That we never needed when they were around; because they were the crazy glue for all of us

     -They bound all the sides together- gently

   And in these moments of my waking memories of you

     -I see the flashes of time spent

  Then moved

    Then taken away

      Thinking- perceiving

        That life lost takes life from your own breath

        Ruthlessly

      Painfully   it

       Places

     Silence upon your footsteps

   Confused

 Angry

Hurting

Never understanding why

You begin to believe that that is it

That it is all over...

And as the tears fall unto shadows

And your body cascades to the floor with pain

Accepting your passing

A wave of grace moves through your bones

And you hear their voice inside your heart

"Life never ends my love- it only continues to shift and begin again"

He reminds her to smile

- reminds her to see clearly

Flashing moments into clips

-softly

Your love shines unto the pieces

Remembering your light

Existing in all of us

And when I cry too much

You are there

With a warm hand to my cheek

And a sweet

Loving smile

Reminding me

That you are still around

-In our memories,

Our conversations-my dreams and visions when I close my eyes at night

In our unconditional love for one another

Beautiful

In moments

Tragic in silence

But the pieces that make up the quilt that signifies our family

Is forever strong

Seeking truth behind tragedy- pulls my mind into many directions

Yet patient I remain – until the truth is revealed before my sight

Of exactly how your short lived life

-was taken

Travel

Take notice in the truth of living

Fear nothing

Go on adventures

Be free to choose to go where the wind of your soul dictates

And stop asking so many questions in your mind

I miss the open road- or walking along the shorelines of new places

I miss taking pictures of how others live and love

I need it- it is better than any other thing

I was born to write

I was born to photograph the world

I was born to be an artist

I was born to teach the masses

I was born to truly live.

As the travels my feet find------------

      The moments worthy of remembrance...

I realize that   It is the journey that makes us strong

           It is the journey that helps us truly see

Time to Shift to the — — Stars

Time to drift – eyes on these lips

Mic clips

Got you stuck upon these topics

Dropped

So damn strong

Inspiring galaxies to shift upon

The pounding heads that draw from

Ecclesiastical rifts

Forever pleasing their finest artistic fix

Lights shine now- eyes close now

Bodies groove into actions

Prematurely erected fractions

Surely you thought you were mastering

But a master of cause is where you thought wrong

Actinic symphonies ring past

Capital cities full of magical radicals

Practical, tangible, and invisibly tactical

As I search now- tired of knowing how...

This grammatical nature devastates lyrical terrors

Of fantastical —Mathematical waivers

Oratorical majors, slapping signals for favors

Sucking out the artists flavors

To mask the miraculous, pro-activists that stomp on the clicks that clack, dissect then distract

Watching as the mysteries that mentally

Rupture the game changing rarities

Seeing things now from a clear eye view...

Senses telepathically designed

Regenerating every cell the instant I close my eyes

To the universe that exists inside

Bodies staying dormant to what is really happening

Gate keepers

Pretending

As we rise... then divide

And lovingly connect to what is the truth... how such truths have always deemed all that was necessary

All that was ever needed to heal.

Once the few can be contained...then the masses can be left to just live

Minus the reliance

Minus the suppression

Minus the hatred

Equality will reign dually

Beautifully, when Sally and Ziana are given the same hand, the same options, and the same types of breaths that relinquish the how- then the why- then the when- before we come back again

This change will make a repetitious cycle disappear- because no one will need it to re-appear

You see

Every generation will create a fair leveled ground

And those that have tried to kill the lights won't matter

The flow of the bringers of the light know

How to see

And their industries will crumble and fade

As humanity creates and entrepreneurs their own enterprise of living

These shifts will be put into the places where their fancy dinners and black suits and guns and bombs will heed

Because the world has had enough

As mothers, daughters, sons realize that pledging their lives to a place of made up control- only leads to more realms of boxes

Minds continue to shift

-As soldiers die, and family ties cry for peace

People wake-

And awake

And awake- and then

Understand the energy collectively as a consciousness creates

A freedom of truth

A freedom of chosen abilities

For it is the truth that always seeks the truth

In tuned – open – minded- soul soldiers

– a gathering for balance to begin to be given

For NOTHING is EVERYTHING and EVERYTHING is NOTHING

Eyes shine through – dimensions

Transmitting reasons

Look to the children – their eyes are the reasons

Clear motions will be understood

As the stars react and move us

Listening intently for messages is a wave of past ideals

Create your own waves

Move your own movements

Lay your own bricks

Rely on no system

But your very own

Star Crossed for Eternity***

Loved ones cross arms

Shoulder to shoulder

Hips clanking towards one another

Strolling towards a midnight dream

Destinations unseen

But so expected and full of life

As they walk

Distantly breath

Beneath the shadows of linear concepts

      Intertwined

Re- a –lining their future footsteps

Sides reaching towards one another's existence

      Nothing else seems to matter any more

And the night sky releases a toxic majesty that liberates even the quietest parts of a man

      He moves closer to her now

      He moves for her

      And she for him

      As one

Dancing – like a couple strolling amidst the essence of a tranquil island breeze

Just waiting for the other

Just holding one another

Content with having the simple measures of a pair linked internally throughout

Creation

Again, and again, and again

They always find a way to remember that they were together before

Dreaming of what it was like

Wishing that sometimes...just sometimes

They could be together freely- minus their spiritual duties

-Guess that's what always kept them blessed- guess that's how their souls continue to manifest

Movements – placed here – to help the masses feel

What they know

Fear nothing and dance more

I can still see it... I can still see you-

Walking with me, sand between our toes, just relaxed

Looking up at the stars in the sky

Ocean breaks in the background

Moons making sense....souls reconnect

Understanding the why

Still tracing me back to the desire to keep the physicality filled

We are full again

And

That is the key

How we move

Who we move

When we move

We are- have- and always will be

Moved to exactly where we must be

For the sakes of what is

Beyond our love

Colors of the Ocean

I remember her eyes

Like the beginning of days

Light and full, sweet and kind

Colors of the ocean

Ran through them like dreams

Glistening amidst the glazed sparkle

-Only; a morning sun could produce

As waves passed by

Crashed and let go

The cylinder beams

Encircling the magic within

Body right as rain

Mind silent and still

Motion subsided and ill attitudes

Turned astray

She was always eager

So full of life

Her energy sparkled

Waterfalls of joy

Insurmountable antiquities

Whispers of a secret passage

To another newly awaited

Unexpected journey

Destination unknown

And hardly foreseen

Yet she always got there

None the less

A storyteller amongst

Disbelievers

A fairy flying amongst fools

But they always did listen, didn't they

To the words that is...

And the path chosen

Was treaded on nimbly

For few had seen the sights she'd seen

Because the feet could

Rarely take you back

To the image surrounding

The dreamers dream

The child's eye

Or the sages divine ability

Reproductions of the great

Yet so simple, it was

And so simple it always can be

To find the path that leads to

The wooded pines

Just beneath the leaves

Fall has dropped between the trees

Light and full and sweet and kind

Are the places

Beside what the imaginations dreams

Making all you love a reality

Even if just for a moment

It was a moment

Filled with ease

Free of struggle

Full of peace

Nothing to worry about

And nowhere important to be

Except for right here

Right now

In this very moment...always and forever free.

Replacing Nothing... Remembering Everything

There are many different types of people in this world

The warm ones

The cold ones

The colorful ones

The powerful ones

The ones full of heart: streaming aurora

Un-swayed

Extraordinary souls

Cherished bliss

The ones whom decide to look after others ------- willingly

The ones that carry with them a familiar sanctity

Of resemblance

-A piece like no other

Irreplaceable fractions held in concave jigsaws

I saw her tonight

A gem hidden in the oceans of time –

Uncovered---- within certain instances

Open enough to see

The mixed between portions of a memory

Holding steady

The reactions held true

With balance, curiosity, and ease

Surviving pieces for us all to look upon

To understand

Beneath all the chaos and attributes of this world

One must suffice

One must conjure up such feelings

Once known

-Then shared- then spread

Amongst granites of tabulates---- streaming artistic musings

Weaving patterns – strung through dealings of hope

Exquisite precious resistance- ones residing in truth

The uprising of a cause

The freedom of the wave

The tumbling crash of water droplets that form within the waterfalls

Surrounding

Moving

Connecting

Still

It is the beginning of the end that simply passes on –

Existing- reacting- bouncing between

Everything

As humanity seeks

A future of meaning

A future of purpose

Full of actual justice led by absolute truth

For the eyes of healing

See the green coated destinies ---waiting to be given

There is indeed much to be done

Awareness transpires

Supplanting the motion

Towards a place of divinity

Residing in our ability

To exemplify unity

-the poor

-the working

-the rich

-the elite

-the brave

-the wise

-the holy

-the shunned

-the majestic

-the proud

-the false

-the true

THE BEAUTIFUL

-Don't we all have something in us that is of light and beauty?

Noticing such is precisely such

Our most imperative lessons-in front of our very noses for the choosing

A multitude of decisions effecting frequencies of division

Cascading sounds

Resonating freedom

That already was and is before your very feet to ascertain

Can you see it?

Riding the wave home to who you are –

Your true selves

Your deepest passions

And never letting that go or fade from your soul

There is a reason you feel it so intensely- consistently

Time and time again

Dreams are here for a reason

Follow them

Don't resist or sacrifice them

They are the places where true happiness lives, grows, replicates

Like the pulsing of your heart

The vibrations of your being

It is here that you shall find paradise

Seeking the natural portions

Then deciding...

Once chosen

Manifested it becomes –reality

As we travel and move

We realize how close we all already are...

Seeking outside of ourselves comes with the notations of experience

Daunting us to repeat what is familiar

Effecting junctions of our perspective – bridged by our choice

Stay and repeat or run and leap?

What is it that is holding us back?

Is it fear...is it responsibility?

Is it a locked in ideal that there is only one way?

Find your own way –create your own landscape– a place in your own time– of your own design
free of the restraints of this place in this time

Know your strength by choosing to live the dream your heart dictates

Then build it infinitely...

How....?

By deciding to   Simply   Begin

Fairy Tale Drops on Pages Unseen

I dream inside the vastness of imagination

    A cabin beside a stream

    Of lush forests

Large, thick trees surrounding my view

As I lean back now

Against the bark...my mind begins to silence

And I am able to be quiet inside- be still and silent inside

Feel the ages of the tree beside my back

    A cool breeze follows this dream and takes my feet to a

    Waterside as my fingers reach down and touch the glittering beams

    Of the riverbed my eyes glance over at a shining pink flower

Gleaming towards the sun's rays

    I follow my feet into the fall of night

I lie in a field of green pastures and look up at trillions of stars upon me- too beautiful

If only you could imagine

I close my eyes now and breathe....slowly

It is now that my heart is at rest

For it is here where I belong.

Sanctuary

When I was young I met this beautiful man, beside the lake

Felt like a dream empowered by once existing

There were no tears in this place

No fear or sorrows shattered by grief

It was new

Fresh- constant

Full of laughter

And relived – each day through

A blissful memory

That meant more to me than I could have ever imagined

It was a connection

It was you

It is me

And as the lake changed

From blue – to orange- yellow to pink

So did the sun

And his eyes never stopped looking

Because it was believed

That every word spoken was true

And although I knew that day would not last forever…

I desired to change what was missing inside

With closing my eyes- then washing it all away

Into something and someone

I forgot how to be

And now he's not with me, but on another side of the lake

A side that I cannot cross into

Yet cannot walk away from

All I can do is stand by it

As still as the trees

And wait for the sails

To converge

Wait for the touch that I have so longed for

To unfreeze the chill

Of a vacant memory

And begin to remember- the day

By the lake – in my dreams

Encompassing Enchantment

Encompassing

Enchantment

Beams spectacles

A fool who thinks he can see ----cannot budge from his prison held cage

For a slave to its space he needs

Like the yearning for one more taste

One more waste

Of his existence ----bearing witness to it

And the changes in his truth

As she watches silently----respectfully witnessing

Demeanor dissipates

Mirror masks

Of glory flasks

Reddened sun

Eyes bloodied by choices chosen

Liquefied by dreamers stances

Of false believed prophecies

Unhealthy droplets consuming lost sight

Flight no longer plight

-ignorance LOST souls

Transpose – hopefully containing more someday

More than this

Better than this

- I know your soul so much better than this-----

All encompassing

Choosing

To morph

To break-

Then practice what you already know

Pouring back now ---- into the depths of your bleeding heart

Time Traveler's Ways...

Sometimes I want so much more than what's here;

What's before my feet- or far away- yet visible beyond the distance of the worlds between it all

And yet I feel so grateful to be alone and in the silence of today

At peace

And whole; and one

It's like a novel waiting to be read

Or pages hoping to be turned- turned faster with experience, or more slowly due to distraction

So I write, and I follow the openings in my life

I allow the raindrops to produce lemon pop sickle breezes- here now today

I wake

I fall

I subside to whatever and wherever I should be

In this very instant

Today

And I do the same tomorrow yet again

But so differently than before

Like the pen that strokes the marks between the lines of recycled pages

Torn stages and ways yet to be seen

Who are we really is the question at hand for me...

Yet, in essence...what purpose could be more important than ourselves?

I believe that we are not to be disposed of

Nor thrown aside from a life that we were meant to live

A life that we were meant to have

Obtain but never own- live with love-but know its precious qualities internally

It is our choices

And our guides help those choices become clear

When we are ready ---

We follow their lead into the abyss that seems so risky at the time

But always gives us love

At least of some kind

Even if for a moment

It still exists

There

        Right there

    For our eyes to seek – and hold true

It is yet so intriguing that we fear or pull from our true destiny

-When all we need do is trust what we've always known and always remembered to be as it is

Perhaps making it all real is the message

      - Perhaps when we decide to create our own reality- it is then that

            -we are truly free

Doorways...dots and places

If she travels to the end of the world

Into every place and every mind and every dot and every page

If she hop's on every boat

And flies every sky

And touches down upon the sands

It is in her fascination

Of a heart yet seeking

Of a mind still wanting

Of a soul still yearning

For its soul mate to be found

The wise men say

Seek not outside thyself

For happiness resides within

It does

And in all of this time spent yearning for those

For one to see it

She waits

And breathes

Yet swells and pounds

Like a raging stormy sea

Enlightenment

Phases

Droplets

As innocent and tiny

As that of a microscopic lens dictates

She sees him in her dreams

She sees him sometimes when she closes her eyes when she dances

A glimpse

A heart beating a pounding like

A sense

An invisible doorway that's right there

But does it exist here

Then she tells herself to believe

Then she tells herself to move on

Then she tells herself that hope

And strength

And courage

And compassion leads to love

Of all kinds

Yet

Gateways seem closed off

And doorways -untold

Like the sphinx's gate and guard

-the locks of time

Perhaps it is in her energy to draw from

-and back into

To fill up

Then drain

Like the angel in the forest

With the vase- pouring water into wells

-for others to see

I know you are out there still

I pray you find me

At a Glance it became a story:

I once met a girl, sitting beside a train on top of the pipes and pigeons, and benches of pleasure filled nights falling onto sunsets behind her. She watched the lights go from bright to blinking, hollow to full, extreme to poetic or exotic perhaps. Dancing across rails of showcase glass windows, dwindling, fondling; falling down- her eyes were dark and sunken far into her skull, following substances dropped along their way home to the forest of consequences and dots.

I asked her where she was off to. After all, the forth train had just passes and she continued her sitting on urine stained sidewalks of pity, thinking foolish thoughts and words, creating walls. A whispering voice peered from below her, or at least it seemed, but in reality she was not speaking. If she was I could not tell.

I thought to judge her, place her, to mistreat her. She said to me, "Child you've never seen what I've seen." Kicked out, thrown aside, cups of change down sewer filled holes in the ground, not far off, or behind, or beyond that voice.

She never did ask for anything; no money, no change- no remorseful offerings. She simply gestured for comfort, conversation, and warm eyes. Not cold features and meek hands of solutions or symptoms of hateful games.

She tried explaining, provoking, disregarding – as I the girl with pieces and clusters

and fragments of things asked her if she needed help. She told me her name. It flowed like

her hair, dreaded with beads and years of experience. She was beautiful, even the prettiest

of face or body or style could never match up to what she carried when she stood up to that

train, that light, that x-bearing sign of yellow and black glows.

Entranced by her tranquility I had forgotten anything I've ever considered to be

important. I walked away from that train; she hopped on without concern of where exactly it

was going, trailing pieces of dignity which became imprinted in the cement. Resembling this

image in my mind: holding out hands to the world, crooked lines on jagged edges. She

proudly didn't follow a certain pattern or schedule or life- encouraging the ability to express

everything without speaking a single word.

This woman I looked up to carried something with her in each step. Her inner beauty

was expressed through her disposition. She released an aura of perplex combinations,

comparing to none I have ever seen. Her style followed no category but her very own,

perhaps in essence- it is our courage to be ourselves that speaks volumes.

This treasured palace holds so many moments

Clung onto and released out of

The soul

Beauty held in our memory bank, so sweetly

With hopes and pleasures

Imaginations of more

An inkling of understanding – past the confusing times where we must ask questions

Sometimes too unsure of how to answer

Sometimes not

But, yet they remain

A part of our minds

And what of the mind

Is it a place that can corrupt the soul if we so let it?

Is it a place that wrinkles the ways of the heart with defeat before we ever try to move past it's ever changing mazes and obstacles of time?

Is our purpose clear?

In faith – we walk

-Reminding ourselves that all shall be -------------what it shall be

And that all we need do is trust and love and live our lives eloquently

So softly spoken at times

So roughly crude at others

And here in the whirl winds of life

We tumble

So many times

Until we switch-

But there are moments where even in the simplest of times,

It is hard to keep our feet

Or to hold our heads above the rising seas that mean to suck the breath from our lungs

With ease

But it is our to struggle- to fight- to paddle and swim and kick harder and harder

To survive

That is but one of the feats of living

And when completed has a sense of peace

A sense of reassurance and truth

Binding us to the trinity that separates us

Asking only asking

Praying oh yes, praying

For reassurance that all that we carry will not always feel so very heavy

And our minds can rest

While our eyes see clear

And we begin to trust

We begin again to believe in love

A different kind of love that only letting go can maintain

That only the real ones possess

And so, as it all changes

So does the water, and the river, and the warmth of the sun

The wind and the rains set in again

With the memory of warm fires on our toes and colors that feel fuzzy

So she smiles, remembering the children

She smiles remembering the purpose

Enlightened in the sense of living the life of her choosing

Woke up feeling extra today

Finding more of times retrospective ways

Reflective ways

Harmonizing creations

Molding lifetimes of dimensions

Of a dreamer's dream

Many of which have been buried-

But the dreams contain realms tied to emotions of everything

They always etch their way back

Upon the souls that crave more

You see they never fade

Fires ignited, souls inspired, cognoscente implications transpired

The lights dim now, eyes seem closed now, hearts beating proud now

I can hear how

The talent that's inside

Paints pictures in my mind

Things flash as I remember

Skyscraper dialects

Free styles manifest

Formulas and equations

Lights forming new types of conversations

Eyes dissecting pervasions

As we watch worlds consumed by havens

Of what's real, a dream so close that you can touch and feel its chance

Its prevalence, its validity because you know in the depths of your soul that it's the truth...

I watch those I have loved stand now

Patient

Deflating egos their previous dictation

A minds finite fixation

Facing; what's deep

The roots of one's heart

Build new foundations, inspiration runs below subway stations

Resonating souls

As ciphers build blows

Amidst foes and

Amidst stages

More moments inside phases

Of a mind left to familiar rages

So....I ask you this now...

Who will you choose to be?

If all we have is

One life, one love, one formality...

Amongst sheep seeking normalcy

Can you lead or will you stray?

When called upon the wise can you stand with pride... knowing that legislation might castrate all that you built knowingly for a reason?

You see it's not about seasons or lifetimes.

What is written, poetically driven, systemically implanted can't be deleted...

They have tried to run us farther astray

But still we rise

Dually

Artists cannot be erased from the time frames concealed by enemy's shields

Our voices resonate on dialects that hold the powers of vibrations past down unto our psyche

Forever shown

Even when at times it seems distracted

We know exactly how to extract the roots our souls reside in

Some how

Some way

Our messages are vessels of the sea

Oceanic waves form

Like tsunamis

Wiping out, cleansing, healing, nations against ternaries eyes

With reasonable ways

Bond by love

Bond by totems

Bond by universal equalities

Bond by our God's dualities

Synchronistic ally

To sanctify

Our memory of why we are here

Why what we do -what we say -Why we live the lives we believe

Why we are who we are purely

Why we believe in what matters in every situation or circumstance casting away the underlying emotions tied to fears that cause our hearts binding

We are profound with spiritual essence,

Its formulations of transgressence

Flow inside chords streaming auroras

Artists rising now- expressing melodies

Heartfelt poets musically, dually providing a way when at times felt like there was none...

So search now, it is time to remember and follow how

The creators that have left us with symbols to understand

The law of a better land

A better man

A better will

To choose what is real.

What is just, what lies in the truth of our souls will never require a documentation to be written; because it is simply known,

In the depths of our being

In the enlightenment of our conversation

In the belief that we all deserve a fair chance

How can we sit here and choose to place one another in boxes

When we have never chosen to walk in another person's shoes, nor have we experienced their pain?

So seeing past the obvious

And leading yourself into your passion, you see that life is beautiful,

That life is a gift

Every human being, child, person, can glow

Does glow

But especially shines- especially when given the way to be who they truly are...

There is no playbook for- noticing it, watering it, and allowing our youth to find it-

It's already engrained

So take a minute to understand-

That understanding people

Makes a world of difference... everything has to start from caring about everything... not just looking like we are, but showing that we are

And unity, it's already there... when we collectively are ready to see past what we think we know- and be open to the possibility that we don't know it all.

It doesn't matter what age you are, what title you have, what job you possess for now...

For what truly matters is tied to none of these things

The reliance on things is the control that creates only an illusion

An illusion whose reality only exists because so many need it too

But only; if we so choose let it

When you choose to be free of it

The sight becomes clear; enlightened and home is felt- connected- tied to everything and everywhere

We all of us are tied to each other

Next one is dedicated to my profoundly amazing little brother: Thomas Brandon Cowling.

May you always remember that- even when times seem hard, cruel, or disappointing- or as the anticipated course changes- that all of the pieces equate unto the definition of your journey. Your adventure may have never happened if other things didn't also happen. Look at life as an endless sky of possibility, unconventionally- free of the constraints of society. I believe that it's then that we are truly happy. I think this life is more than work, or land-, or possessions. For I have come to realize that -it is the moments that we have in life that define our souls. Our humanity, our love, and our ability to choose to live a simple life exists' within us all. I used to think I had to do A, B, then C before I could begin living any of my dreams. It was only from the unexpected parts- that I began to realize how we at times can become our own worst enemy. Blindsiding our abilities- limiting ourselves because it is almost a habitual pattern in this place... Listen to your spirit, my dearest brother- you have a whole life to live – an entire world to see and explore, accompanied by your grandest of stories to tell. I believe in you, and I love you so very much!

There once was a man filled with so many things

The best of ideas glistening

He had a white beam of light that flowed through his crown

An anchor that held his feet firmly to the ground

And a cord tied to the depths of his soul that awakened his senses- when he was young and when he was old

Some nights he would dream, and struggle and strive

Some days he felt like something was missing inside

And when nothing seemed to feel like it fit,

He'd walk along the shores of his mind for a bit

Searching for answers to questions and ways

Searching for freedom, love, and a happy place to stay

The simple things in life made him feel free- and

His joy was most known when he used his imagination to see

It opened up doorways that led to his heart

His intelligence was strong, and so was his heart

And as he at times worked himself bare,

And the mountains seemed to grow between him and his cares

He'd close his eyes and remember to dream

Of the world that lived

Inside the pages in-between

He'd see the compounds broken down molecularly

Generating, and regenerating vastly

And as he observed the smallest forms of life

He noticed how relevant and beautiful life can be

When the rays of the sun, and the roots of the tree

Dive deeply

Connecting to realms of energy

And when he felt lost

Or alone, or astray he would wander about

And cast his line into the sea

And one night he decided to walk by the stars

Kicking the rocks that held the secrets to mend others hearts

He stumbled and fell on something he didn't see

Lying on the sand next to the shore inside his dream

He picked up that thing that caused him fall

A stone with imprints and a majestic call

Its messages pounded like the beating in his chest

His fingers ran gently across its ridges with rest

Knowing, somehow sensing its familiarity

Touching the lines engrained on its back

Noticing the smooth sections

That remained intact

For this stone was no ordinary stone, you see

For this stone, it had seen many days

This stone had traveled from one shore to the next

Was picked up and thrown

Putting its will to the test

As the oceans and creatures moved it from place to place

This stone witnessed more than most would ever taste

And as he held it in his hand

Ease began to fall upon his mind

He smiled realizing the emblem within the grains

The etchings engraved over time from the waves

The energies validity existing in times fine graces

Yet at that moment something inside him felt strange

A fear that grew inside the man's questions

Then doubts

I am no stone and I don't deserve to be thrown about

He wanted to throw it into the sea

And as he was about ----to fling away --------such a powerful entity

The sky began to grow and move and then shift

And things began to change ever so swift

The waves before him became darker and felt strange

The window he looked out of grew distant and brief

As the mist grew heavy around his feet

His body became old, and dark, and then gray

His bones became meek, then crumbled one day

Afraid and alone he called out to the sky

Asking and begging for a reason why

And just when he thought that all had gone away

A voice whispered to his spirit and struck a chord in such a way

That the man could not deny noticing a change

The mists of the sky answered the man

With a message inscribed within the depths of the sand

I gave you gifts to remind you of things

I gave you the visions that lay inside your dreams

I watched from afar as you experienced pain

-But plans that are not based upon your dreams-

----Can crumble like bones in the ground----

--Void of the passion embedded inside the grains--

-Decompose and grow old...

-Not because they were not real-

--And not because you did not heed-

------------------------------But rather ----because you must see,

Then choose to follow what your heart truly craves

I watch you humans living for a future, forsaken by a past

Stuck in a cycle that does not last,

For moments are moments

And days are days

And it is the passion of living in them ----that makes it the journey that you crave

You see,

Old we become when we turn out our light

Old we become when we give up true sight

You are here now because it is time for you to choose

You are here now to remind you of the stones deep hues

Whose marks had not been made; had it chosen not to budge

The man looked down at the stone in his hand

He noticed its grains that were etched from the sand

----The lines definition created from the waters it grazed

Made from the beatings and poundings of waves

--------As well as the smooth touch it contained

The man looked at the sky and smiled inside

Realizing the depths inside the story one little stone had made

It was in that very instant the man opened his eyes

Holding that stone, firmly in his hand

The mist gently dissipated – and carried him away

And as the man traveled into new lands

It was then that his story grew miraculously

The precise instant he chose to reach for the sky

It was in this space that he felt love inside

Watching the sun set from the peaks that rose above

Internally he wasn't sure if life would always go his way

Holding onto it all

For his sense of freedom was never too far away

He could live, change, break, fall, make mistakes, design glory- all the while

Sculpting the mountains forged from the courage of his heart

For the rock and the stone and the sand and the water all carry with them

His lessons and his memories

Beautifully crafted from experience

Just as no two people can have the same destiny

No two stones will ever feel the same

In his hand

On that day—

And as the water that smoothes the stone

And the ridges it creates

Connects the ties that bind

All things...melodically-rhythmically—harmoniously

Within the sands of time

For eternity

He realized... so then does his soul.

...

Daydreams subside

As travelers glide unto places unseen

Beyond the mundane chosen constriction

Surrounded by love

      Are those who show love

Just as light seeks light

And as images flash through my mind

Written

Spoken

Seen

Foreseen-unseen

Then re-rooted ------to ------------------carriers

              Of messages

                       ------------All becoming ------intertwined

Into symbiotic melody

Synching sounds-----------that resonate -------AWAKENING

The signs of each -----------entity

Of love

How it works ---is

Beautiful really...

We write

We speak

We create ---more than we realize

Pulsing drum beats

And lyrical shift shakes

What we write is the very thought of one another's souls

As she listens

Noticing how

Pairs of certain things are linked infinitely

The very definition encompasses its divinity

To recognize it

To respect it

Is the very link to all forms of life

And the love it all creates -----------interjects waves

And forges new levels of connectivity; ones aligned with grace.

Blessed by a Child

Her tears rolled like raindrops from a falling pane

Sun setting glimpses enticing poetries reigns

Distilled, silent, pure-unspoken

Absolute truth radiating eyes

I remember the night falling

The whispers inside my mind

I remember the door close

I saw the glass break

Frozen in time

As the shadow crept into my soul...

I heard the cracks within

The sound of a human's heart crushed and backed up again...

Racing oh so fast

To keep up with these times

Angelically awaiting – a peaceful way to shine

From a world left without hunger, pain, or disbelief

A world where the lights pass down oh so deep

A world filled with love and compassion in between

Where broken is but a memory

Taken by the sea

Knowing

Oh yes knowing

That my sweet soul shall be set free...

And the purity in their eyes contains a world within

Emotion overwhelms every – single-ability

When they told you   you could

Not   win

For the challenges of my heart

Move in all things- in a multitude of directions

Connecting to what flows strong and deep

Wisdom shakes

Beauty basks

I see your eyes my dearest sweet

Your innocence spreads

As I watch you grow

I realize how much each of you mean to me

I thank you for every gift, every moment, and every memory

You brought life back to me

You reminded me

Inspired me

Ignited in me

The light inside imagination

Creating ---the definition ---of living ---what happiness means- to never go through the motions of settling for a life you do not love--- the expression you carried was perfectly contagious

Thank you ---for helping me remember ---precisely ---what I needed to know.

-Thank you Charlotte Rose

The locusts remind her of time

Locusts that only she can hear

The souls from the purest of things
Something beautiful remains, within this place

Do they see it and hold it as dearly as the dimensions of eternity?

Healing passions coming through the streams of lifetimes and sanctions of grace

Forests of knowledge projecting waves of exactly what is necessary for a calling...

A way that makes marks upon pages, and a reason for what the definition of truly living contains

Do not get caught in the webs of practicality

Do not lose sight of one-self

Do not forget to truly remember

Do not forget to search – and take notice of natures qualities

    ---for it is then that you can go back to what matters again

    In every direction chosen

As the ocean makes its sounds and the dragon flies fly – and the seagulls drop into it- then glide then fall then rise - so do the motions of each life

The peaks of life kiss the crests of solidarity

Confined no more

Free as rain

Shining beyond what was real...unto a realm of what one can see...

There is no space

There is no time

There is no palace of aggrandized gestures in between

There are moments of love beneath the sand

Written in the pages of our memories

Tongues that stretch beneath our hearts to speak of every single beautiful story

There is no wrong or right in this place

Only love

Soaring past glimpses of a dream long lived

A dream that is wrapped in all of who we are- watered by all that we believe---limitless of mind; and as familiar as the divine mate of our soul.

Beams

For the moon and the wolf

The rising unto ends

Bring light for told

Beginning, once more again

Like the pounding of waves that cry unto men's souls

Awake and alive

We rise like sunbeams

While dipping our toes into luminescence

Its passing love

Craves substance

Guided winged tailed dreams

Dreams that creak open

Gateways

The dreams that begin under a desk lamp in a

Brown-stone from afar

Not noticing the philosophy

Dropped

From such a windowed pane

---Converge and see---------------------------

How similar all lines of divinity

Create

Canvases of pure poetry

Music

Songs that sleep always dream

Songs awake rupture screams

As the maker lays to a peaceful rest

His music is preparing for its best

Moments left till they awake

Together reborn, a mission will partake

Within these thoughts spirits manifest

A beautiful phrase that releases all the stress

For this life you contain is simple and true

I want you to know there lays a piece of me in you

Traveling through the seaways of the mind

My heart reaching euphoric causes in time

Presence coincides

I find

Myself

Yearning

To always be near

My souls

Deepest love

So I sleep with peace

So you shall find

Only ease

That flows

Inside

Every level

Of these eyes

Nightly Love

There are moments encountered that feel

As though one has strayed into one of their very own dreams

The warmth felt

The vision captured

And the light that glows beneath

The effervescence of time

I saw this in a young man's eyes tonight

It was almost as if he was waiting for me

Grasping onto my fingers as though he didn't want to let me go-

And yet I don't know why

But I do know what he felt

For I still feel it

Even now

Even inside the chills of this night

He had something

An-energy about him

And it waits within my bones for the dealing

Powerful and untamed – ripping past the currents within the curl of that dome

Crashing into shallow waters that carry within them a peace... I'm yet to know and unleash

Empower and understand

Perhaps I will get to know you

Perhaps not

We shall see

But something about those eyes will be remembering me

And I enjoy the thought of that

In fact it's quite soothing

And you were rather

Intriguing...the mystery let go of – felt but never had-

A love I feel I remembered

Even though I never saw you again; I learned looking back now- that what we see- who we meet- what is known- never goes away.

And love is love- and even if that one remains a mystery- inside I am content with knowing that in one of my lifetimes I was lucky enough to have had it.

Butterflies Guiding Grace

Want for nothing

Need for nothing

Live life for yourself

Yearn not for love- but have love know your love

For when you live a life full of love- it picks up particles of it

Just as the stone is scraped by the sand- then smoothed by the water

Burnt by the flame

Then cooled by the wind

The stone yearns not for comfortable places-

The stone's life resides in its ability to morph, and change along the way

A reflection of all its markings – yet in still a stone just the same

It yearns not to be loved

For it is love

It forgives its trials- and bows its head in gratitude for the next wave

Pounded into the sand or not

Smoothed by the water or not

Floated by – for the sake of a turbulent wind

It is then re-rooted into the Earth

The stone continues to move-

And continues to love every cycle- every step- every dream- every loss- every ounce of joy along the way

For that is life- and life comes with lessons until we are ready to see----them all

With a line- up of new ones to forge

And in time understand

Want for nothing

Need for nothing

Live life for yourself

Yearn not for love- but have love know your love

And just as you think that the tides you see become a distinct part of reality

The water will shift – seem calm- maybe even lead you astray

But your soul soldiers will fly in –and guide your heart that day

As frail as the butterflies wings- foretold...

Lye in such tiny spans

The motions...

To glide over rough seas

An eccentric pattern embedded through the mist

So bright – yet so subtle

Only certain eyes may see

Home is this way

As he flutters effortlessly towards the direction inside

Instilled

Flowing

All the way home

BLUE
SKIES

Blue skies

Swells barreled perfection

Sun beams of delight

She smiles

Knowing

Exactly what she has

Is right here

Inside

Options are all around us

Every single day

Choose to see them

Choose to love them

Choose to love yourself – enough –more and more

With each passing day

Each sunset you are blessed enough to see

Each mountainous peak climbed – holds lessons of songs sung

By what the beauty of nature holds

Tied –linked – closely now

To all of the aspects of her dreams

Thankful for it

Remembering all of it

Feeling all of it

Because she must – be complete

And in so – she is completely free

Nothing can stop her not now

Not ever

She resides in the eyes of purity

Sees the stones deep hues

Listens to the lessons of her ancestors

Her bloodlines – their majesty

But mostly she remains true

And that my friend's

Is all you need ever do – to reside in the motions of your imaginations sanctity

Church bells sound in the distant rain –

Reminding us now....of the strength the sun contains

The beauty of one's brain

We are one...we   are   one

                                        Can you see the blue skies?

Can you see they are a reflection of our love?

Collectively... projecting our hearts and the depths that our hearts contain- are vulnerable- yet true – and that passion is conceived in a place only you can touch, reach, and show- only you

Only you can choose your truth.

It's beautiful how much you can fall in love

With the essence –sounds

Ones voice

That single sound

Connects

So many

Memories

But at the same time

Is precisely how technology

Inhibits – multiple ways to connect- depends how you use it-

Our

Humanity

Replacing space forms

With something less

Emotional

Something less beautiful

Something less tied to what moves us

The sounds of our voices carry meaning

The sounds of our souls are transpired within each movement, every vibration, not to be taken away

Remember why we make sounds

Remember the melody – and passion behind every single word you choose to speak

Its presence resonates and should not be disconnected from the world but heard via the tools of technology

Remember that the tools are not here to divide us and isolate us- use them to connect our voices- wisely...

While also knowing when to put them aside and share in the moments of those present right now.

Circumstances of Living

It starts with a beginning

There in choosing to begin a story of your own design

Its entity streams from a power within –a place only one can get to – in time

Surrounding yourself –with – yourself

–Knowing the depths of your journey within such ....helps you see, clearly

–Cause I see now

Our love has been like the sun –I see the North Star in the sky up above

I feel your heart growing –every single day, my circle encompasses...entities of grace

Tongues passed down 'n

  Channeled

Subscribed and unseen

It's like the leaves that grow into pastures and waves insurmountable

Yet free

I break free

I see clearly what freedom is

And contains

Poetry – artists

Jobs that may seem common to most

Hold so much sway on the world

And every time I try to force myself or try to force my heart and soul to conform

Back to what seems like

A state of rest

Cascades into mountains of conquest

Conformist am I none

A normal life I won't contain

                Free

To travel inside the melodies of my brain

Music

Rhythm

Dance   brush strokes throughout time

Sky dive through – white rafting – jungalistic –remote cabins unspoken too

And so you hike up that mountain and feel the gorge of is peak

You remember – you see

The meadows that unfold through the trees that they graze

The life inside every single cell

And the connection of it all

I challenge you all as well as I challenge myself

Can you choose to not be like the rest?

Can you choose to not fall victim to this wicked concept of a life that has been forced upon
frameworks

You see –the foundations of creation were never built upon this world or this place

They were made

To help the messages hold meaning

And as the masses pretend to feel comfortable in their own skin – this feeling desires to
multiply like a plague

Until everyone notices to cover their mouth and put up their shield and FLOW
ANYWAY

If everyone was unleashed from this circumstance of living

Perhaps there would be more giving

And the dreams that line the subway stations

Of the in-between

-Perhaps that's why God put musicians in the tunnels

Perhaps every dimension has a gateway and a door

And only when we are ready to see it – does it open and restore

Our deepest questions

Our familiar ties

Our ancestor's tongues

The stories that they've cried – passed down through cultures unseen

Dually – noted as – a majestic place –in-between

Animals can see it

-so can kindred souls

Stars remind us of universes untold

Yet we flow

The existence of it all is there

When we open our minds to see – it's then

The truth unfolds

Like the wings of a beautiful butterfly

Who never knew how beautiful it was

-Envied

By the solar plexus' above

Moving oh yes moving – oh so fast it seems

Waves of gravity rotating

But yet it's still a dream

For ties and locks inside

Every

Single

Soul

Accompanied by how lucky we are in life

We can find each-other and progress by shedding light

Unto to the others – beams of light

Perhaps our mission is odd in its quest

-Perhaps our mission doesn't require any tests----

But only feeling within the gut of our souls

Rhythmically moving

Unto places of purity

I see now why

　　　Every lifetime and experience of what I've traveled through means

I see now the reasons of struggle or heartache and pain

I see now the reasons of knowing who you are – just the same

And none will I settle

Not today nor after

And that strength coincides with the dimensions your soul transpires

For every lesson learned is a lesson gained for the universe to grow to

May we learn from each other

May we seek better days

May we breathe and rest and know

The love that our hearts contain and even if

We are not sure

Look inside and see

Know that guidance is everywhere

CAN YOU SEE?

Much love to you all

Much love to your dreams

Unfold your hearts

Smile at the beauty it contains

Bow your head – then look up at the sun

Knowing; that you are closer to the divinity of one

A Trembling World

The waters came tumbling in without warning

Fear struck the world of our unknown consciousness

Or recollection that holds any sort of relevance

And the world felt the shakes and screams

Like darkness creeping on the souls unsaved

We craved for much- but lose the rest

In the crowded shroud of nobility without reason for belief

Our destruction may arise – in due time

The ground has with stood about all it can manage at times

Before the struggle – came control

And because of the surrounding bubbles

They've lost the soul of the earth

The one that speaks to us in our dreams which at may have no means of survival or
understanding

But yet they are there

Waiting to be found – listened too – and remembered

For what they are

For who we are

So why do we constantly try to escape truth?

When in the dyer end all that remains is our real spirit

Our real soul – divinely

Connected to a world unseen but existing with each breath

And step taken towards our actual peace and place in this world

In this time

I look back and know the pain, the sacrifice, and ask the heavens for their wisdom and guidance

To protect me from the shadows

On my path

So strenuous at times – yet so beautiful at others

It makes me curious as to whether the decisions I've made have been the ones I needed to choose

Or grow into

Or become

Is she real- or is she a lying fool...beside herself in a pool of bliss and misconception

Is there strength enough to fight what is yet to come?

Does she have the courage to respect politely the selfless deeds before her?

-Or crumble into the worlds of destruction surrounded by chaos with so much to live for and so much to become?

The soul must let go of the guilt and the shame – because it is not and never was her fault

The only peak now is accepting and overwhelming that and believing in the wolf that fights the others insides

And I believe that our power animals will win- then guide our souls to a passage of safety and freedom

For it is such a rare thing in this place

And always was easy to forget with the cloth pulled up over the eyes

Shielding the inner silence- because in life and living that is all you will ever need

The ability to quiet the games of the mind

Then choose to fulfill your true destiny by the means you choose- you create- every feeling and control every reaction.

Awakening the Ancients

Pieces of memories belong to different things

The spirit is quiet and waits to be told

Waits for the wind to subside in the east

Waits for the waves to crash amongst what's next

For it can never truly be fully understood at times

Not even by the most wise

Not even by the most prophetic dreams

Even when they happen we sometimes forget what they mean

I foresee a future that is guided by those close to me

On all levels

On all plains of reality

And dimensions unseen

They've been waiting and resting-- for quite a long time

For they have heard my heart calling to the divine

And now so inspired yet so silent I sit

Working and weaving the minds un-rested resistance and re-acquaintance with my ancient ones rising

The Earth

My great friend and provider

I climb upon you –beside you and with you in these confusing times

Hoping that your wisdom shall guide me and protect me

Please dear souls of mine

The spirits and fairies and angels that surround me

I believe in your abilities and pray that they too shall influence mine

I am grasping my power and understanding my fate

Considering my choices – along the path you all wish for me to take

So with this––– I desire one task––– and one alone

I ask for your protection

And to stand near me when I am alone

Because there's something that stirs deep within my chest

Something that tells me to be alert and not to rest

For the change has come and it comes upon us swift

Like the oceans grave power or the storms covering drift

Courage remains inside the depths of our truth

Fear no darkness my dear sweet child

The wisdom lies within you and always has

Like the pasts blood

   - Entities of other worlds-

Fighting separating

Kindred

Our strength is within all that is good and green and pure

Rising unified percussions

Connective

Love

Images flash through my mind

Written

Spoken

Seen

Foreseen

Unseen

Then re-routed

To the carriers of messages all becoming intertwined

Into symbiotic melody

Synching sounds that resonate

AWAKENING

The signs of each entity of love

How it works

Is beautiful...really

We write

We speak

We create

More than we realize

Pulsing drum beats

And lyrical shift shakes

For what we write ———————is the very thought of one another's souls

As she listens to his words that she had previously written alone

And did not share

But pairs of certain things are linked so infinitely

It's an awestruck divinity to recognize

To respect

Like all forms of life

The love it creates

And the love it all creates

Interjects waves

And forges new levels of connectivity

Ones aligned with grace.

Dawn of Life

So it is here

In the dawn of this life

        That we are discovered

And our time is decided

    In the form of our own stories

And within each story is a feeling that carries the power of us all

Combined to form a pattern   in the dimensions of time

To be forever shared among our pages, bindings, and words

Each one- began with a feeling   so strong   that we chose to write it down

And when it is written

All is formed- takes shape

We are

  Simply what we are

But we are beautiful if

We are true

Within these spreads of time

  Lies significance

Among our thoughts and deeds

    It is what we do that determines who we are

Even though the wise may seem to have all the knowledge ----

　　It is their wisdom that does not always give an answer

To what it is we seek presently

Our whole lives we strive for perfection

But inside of that is a bubble that contains all we are

And all we love ·

And outside the bubble we seek the answers

But it is only when the inside is breached that the answer is given

To no longer look for what you seek

But know that it has already been found

Inside the dome

We build inside ourselves

The wisdom of all our fathers from every age – along with the guidance of all the mothers of our times

Here – on this Earth

Is contained deep within ourselves and

Every day we become that much closer to it　　　　　again

It was always there to begin with – when you begin to live – and open up- and see

But – mostly believe – in your direction

It is our beliefs that give us our strength

To never stray from them

To always keep them close to our hearts

That dome

This space

Stories telling

The understanding

Within me day by day we find a way

Can We Give

And so she reached with hope

Filled eyes of pure innocence

Towards

The purple that sprung from the green

She picked it

And gave it to those who needed it most

Those who were filled with the most gruesome troubles and despair

Not because she was asked

But because she was told

By something that does not take shape, nor have a distinct form

It simply was——invisible

It was within this spectrum of time that our thoughts may meet our actions

For it is not how long we live

But what we do with our life

In each life

As it is given to us graciously

Within the choices of our lives and the stakes set before our very feet

Do we choose to climb the steps of the mountain side?

Or fall deep into the oblivion of existence?

    -By simply existing...

It is but a whisper

On the breath

Beneath

Our spirits

True nature

And inside of it lies ------------------------------BELIEF

So strong that even when strayed from

We know

That we stayed away from exactly where we belong

      We find

                 Spirit

In the faces of those we least expect – something

Meaningful

      Where it lies – is often at times right beneath our noses

Right in front of our eyes decent

The freedom of understanding

Its gifted motions of creativity

Fluidity

Showing

The world's synchronicity

Contained

     Some may say that it is time   others may say it is not

Stand and be silent?

Strike and move...

Or sit and be still?

    It is for your conscious to dictate – pushed out unto a collective consciousness- a belief in what is known

Indivisible

     Such a vision remains unseen by some   while open to few

But it is there

And so are we

So is this Earth

And we must

Recognize the choices

Can we pick the purple that sprung from the green... and give it to those who need it most?

There are times in a person's life that appear hazy and unseen

And all that we thought we knew

Was of no thicker substance

Than the air – we breathe

    Lightly overthrown by

      What one instant may change – one crush of a winding cycle

A whim

A spectacle of lights

Or a simple close of one's eyes

Our beauties glow from time to time

Some subtle- others free

Upon what we dream and desire – to someday have

And the people – our friends

Our people we have – we must hold tightly and embrace and love

For our time with them and their moments

Move as quickly as the way we felt that one time-how it seemed to be tied into the imprints

Of memories keys

The lessons we try so desperately to instill

And the minds of our children
The world's beings – are truly

Amazing creatures

And all we need do is care about the importance one life makes
The sentence spoken before we believed it to be the end

Inspiration may at times be difficult to see
But when it becomes clear and life becomes living
You realize
You begin
To believe
And see-
The molecules connected to the particles which are part of what gives us the ability
To breath
Which is in still a place within a person- whose insight to the world is like a progression

This everlasting desire to push forward
For our cause is part of who we are
Not only to ourselves
But to each other

Waking dreaming seeing releasing fearing falling sinking swimming living transitioning

Waking dreaming the space between——

And somewhere—— along the way   you reach down and pick up what was missing

You see...

The only way to find our dreams

Within our dreams

Is to dream about what it was too dream.

Transmigration

People jump across planes

And sands of time

To lose memory or recollect there of

To escape the realms laid before their feet

Chaotic glimpses of what they always wanted to forget

Rather than choosing to remember

What it was once like

To live

Their feet touch the grains

Now small pebbles wash along

Glimpses misplaced into that

Other section

Over there

The section of those who want nothing

Feed on nothing

Until the hole becomes so large

They lose themselves into it

And I wish

And I pray

For those ones that became

Divided

Amongst the questions in their minds

To pause

For what rises and falls

Seemingly throwing you into a state of distress

A space of mazes

And closed doorways

Questions residing in a state of feeling as if

Knowing is but a distant blocked off memory

That you cannot seem to get too

More intensity arises

This place of unrest becomes even more uneasy to beat

Blessings though always resided within your heartbeat

Does it take tragedy for people to realize what is real?

Does it take pain beyond any count of reasonable doubt for them to breathe again?

What or whose life does it cost to reveal the truth in their own lives?

Those who wanted to feel free- at times blindly create their own prisons

Within their own minds

Not realizing how free they already are in this very instant

From the beginning

From the dawning of time

Their minds were all it took to change

To forget

To move on

To embrace

To love

To realize

To relive

To give their hearts

To embrace their souls

Every life is worth living

Every dream

Every thought

Has a sound

In time

As our imagination strives for

Fights for

Lives for

Dies for

Creates more

With passion inside

Transpiring our soul's wing tipped movements

Remember that

Remember how beautiful you are

How much beauty surrounds you day by day

In a multitude of ways linked

Entirely to your perception

Of yourself –your heart contains so much love

Its vibrations

Streaming

Pulsating

Changing

Everything

Inside of you

Before you

Ahead of you

But mainly right here

Now

The instant you decide

To stay

Surfing and Falling in Love

The sun it poked through clouds that day

And I remember every

Bit

Of

Love

Felt in that place

On that moment

On that day

It was like...

All of us-were free

It did not matter what time it was

Or anyone's age

Or the trials and tribulations of that very first morning

Everything was clear

Everything was washed away

Healed

And we smiled

And we laughed about life

And it was like

Time

It didn't matter

The only thing that mattered

Was

Catching

The next wave

Paths

At peace

At peace

For once at peace

Waves of silence pass through my body

Now echoing thoughts of melodic bliss

Beautifully intertwined to produce

A healing introspection of

Pure love

No thoughts racing

No heavy pounding

Simply plain

And old and retired yet alive

Like the woman on her porch in the Georgian sun

Peaches blossom and

Seeds fall onto grounds of

Soil and paths – floating now

Dimensions rise and tides form peaks of understanding ways

Cause the world came together today

Because the rain drops came down today

Flourished life of rainbow crossings

Overwhelmed with nothing

Knowing everything

Cause life throws journeys to unseen eyes

So when you stop to try

You realize why

And when you smile instead of frown you realize why

Cause happiness brings the answers and good energy flows

Cause when you sit on an uneasy feeling

It spreads and fumbles and multiplies – until the original way is lost

-Forgotten – not conceived

 And the Earth has not forgotten today

               The Earth was in no rush today

                       And even through the cloudy sky

                 The trees shined green and the flowers flourished ties of stem kisses

To the cheek of a child

Whose innocence wandered until she was tired and fell asleep

To dream about life

Growing past realities dome

Saying —

Mommy look how I've grown – tall and skinny, yet short and deep- my roots touch- down past where most can't see and my legs have brought me to this peaceful land

Where wisdom grows from trees

And candy falls from leaves

As Mommy smiles and pats her head

My baby girl has shown me what I fed

                                    Through my breast

                                              Silky and strong

I know now that life is long

                        Even when I'm gone away

My baby girl will carry my ways and this love I feel – she'll pass along

Until it's time for her life to move on

                  My precious eyes have seen so many gifts

Talent beyond emotional drifts

As time decides to switch

                        Over

                                    Onto the next page

Intense   intense   onto the next phase

Of unity between   those you   love

And unity of those who see above   what's real

Reaching, touching, grasping, believing   in all who come across our path

Even those

Who

Decide to pass

Realizing now that everything fits together somehow

And all thoughts I decide to think

Lead me to a fountain

As I take a drink

Wildly thrown into the fields

Of willow tree bliss

And flowers to feel ----touch

So delicately see ------myself in them

                              And them inside of me

Only

 To smile again knowing

The depths   inside your beautiful

                         Breathtaking life

Release

Water ripples waves

Crescents change

Pasts drawn

As elbows lean————————against a railings end

Brown whispers fade beyond the breeze and bright blue eyes——disappear the fear

Leaning back towards Mama's wing

                              Ripples cease and tides bring ease to those waiting for
the current arrival

Staring down into the nothingness bliss

                      Sage burns sounds translucently fixed

To blow

Fingers to pen——pen to the touch

            Paper marks

–reality drifts

            –So softly spoken

            HER WORDS REACH

Euphoric

 Ends   now   beginnings

Beauty finds

My next step

Pure breaths

The text shows again

Dancing ------joy ------------dancing --------------release

The peace leaves green emblems

Illuminating

-Enlightenment- resting -------------within the art of letting go.

Protective Eyes

Face in sky

As eyes peer

Protection

Through the seas of affection

I lose

Thoughts

In

A

Melodic array of colors

That shined

             Through

                  Your eyes

Like the souls gentle breeze

Caught a butterfly   and forgot about how to try

Just simply did

Sister and brother together we

Severed the

World

Into pieces

Topics dropped

Thought about and discussed because it was real and necessary and true

Composing healing vibrations unto ends we could see through

Feeling

Life...extending

Sage

Bones touch and fingers reach

Souly desiring to meet at the depths of the words you speak

Beauty storms from every corner you bestow

-like a weeping willow...you proceed to show me a small fraction of a thing

So many beginnings

I only wish I knew

How to explain – the connection that rising- in between---- the names of things

Or actions or a song sung sweet

Untouched---- unique

Like the snow – a virgin invisible to a world of eclectic passion

Transforming softly spoken speeds into melodies and remedies

These melodies of peace come-

Close realms held

Proceed into a land unknown together

The working of those chosen shall pass through another generation

Surpassing meanings

Lasting – as for

The beauty we already contain it

We already are able to explain it and I am ready to proclaim it---- if your heart is ready to receive it

It is then that the pictures shall be painted and the brushes shall be drawn with precision Precisely melded within

Close ties

And the moon shall protect it

For it tends to curve and stray from the wild

Our abilities of being free are because of our understanding

-with words beautiful

I release your depths so we can see lyrically and melodically – as one

I reach for your hand to unite a union-

True destinies surpass the meaning behind the feeling

And the feeling behind the meaning

Of being

Walking

Living

- JUST PURELY LIVING -

Igniting a power so strong that all shall hear it and live as one

All shall hear it and live as one

Where human beings remember the codes of HUMANITY

Adia

In love with life

In love with love

Pearling across a crowded room----left empty

To wonder

Where it all goes sometimes

So strong

. So gorgeous ----the sun at its rise

On the back when it's setting

Lying down now

Beauty walks in pages

And ages seize to know the answers why

But they are good and pure and true

I see the love in our eyes

At our fingertips

And smile

Because he's there

To know the troubles of my heart

And my pain

To lie in bed and feel the same

To kiss and touch with emotions so true

The gateway open ----------eyes divide------------then sway forward back into the

Groove

Of something so simple

So sweet --------------so ancient --------------yet--so new

I still blush when he looks at me

Feels me

Becomes me

In an ocean of colorful bliss

------Motionless

We swim together we grow up together

For this I would not give up the world

Because love

Of all kinds

Is hard to find

And I feel I have found a link to something so deep

I smile

Close my eyes and dream

About what will come next...

Money

Colors fading from black white to green

Imprinting

Pigments of lost formation

Codes containing reflections

Buying our way through lost affections

Recollections of how it used to be

Trading some food for some bowls to start eating

Away

Our souls lost

The imaginary path

Plagued with a hunger for green illusion paths

No happiness- in this juggling act

Seeing

Inscriptions of a numbered replication of a government relation – slowly tasting

What it means

To have control over

Those waiting

To go back again

And fade in

To ——its energy

Once created its value forged from a demise of the hearts it has bled dry

Its lies – corrupted even the prettiest of eyes

So why do we value this paper to live?

Why do we see it as the only way to give?

——A person a happy life

Through strife – we may obtain the worthiness of a piece of paper with the Presidents
name....

That remains

A mere fantasy for personal and falsified gain

It's a damn shame

The conspiracy behind the minds of such a game ——

Money.....

Ain't it funny.....

How it's got me.....

Stuck ...

Change the system by creating a new one that works, one void of greed, one founded upon
principle, not monopolized and controlled by the likes of a few-when we all stop using it and
feeding into to it- we will be able to truly be free of its grasp.

As time passes, the memories do none the same...

The loves of our lives remain – forever pushing us onwards

Toward the depths of our dreams

Never alone

Even when it feels like it

We rise

We smile

We cry

We dance

We create – we live and love life –

Maybe it's because to have found such love- then to know the depths of it is such a precious gift

And the memories that were captured

My goodness do they make you smile...

And some days

We wake and realize something...

We begin to see that light inside of our memories – is so incredibly special

Its purity cannot be replicated

And it is the memories that define the etchings and photographs imprinted in our minds eye

Placing always a pathway back to it – like a map when we feel lost

Or a wave of positive emotion that washes through us when we look up, in a way...

We always find our way home-

For our home resides within the love we have known

And the true loves of our lives-

They design pulses that reside in our hearts

Poetically

Beautifully

Unforgettably

And when we find them again

We know them

We feel them from across the room

We are pulled directly into their souls again

Forever more

Forever free

For love always finds love

And love is never lost- perhaps our souls morph, change, move into other realms, but they never go away-

They go where they must but always remember love- and always know exactly how to find one another throughout eternity.

Respecting Natures Purity

Our souls

As pure

As nature

As unforgiving

As what nature can destroy

But

The laws of nature always rebuild, they always find a way ——to make life

Even when

It has destroyed life

But it makes you think if it was ever truly destroyed

Perhaps it was just shifted

Because it was time

Because

The patience

Of nature

Lasts a long while

It never wants to hurt things

But sometimes

It grows tired of   being   taken from

Sometimes it must protect the entity of its nature

Like the life that the ocean... breeds

Like the life that the soil contains

Like the life inside every tree

The air that wants its quality

The birds that want a home

The animals that were here first

You see

Everything is linked

It's time we all respect it

And when everyone does

My God ---that will be ------a glorious day

                    We are moving into that space

And I'll see it

Soon

The Little Things

Time causes

Everything to stop

Becoming

Breathless

        Paused in time

Locked into our minds like a vision seen

Inside

And then

        We release

We let go

        And embrace

Those gifts

Preciously

        -given by the Earth

A Goddess of beauty and love

        She gives us so much

And when we see her – she sees us- and gives us all of her beauty eternally

Her branches reach divinely

　　　For the things that you contain

Are inside heart streams that unwind

Wondrous lives

And the energy

　　　Inside is

Similar to that of a final sunset----a final glance

A wallowing desire in-between-　　　　　just one more phrase

One last glance

　　　Before I close my eyes　　　-and if I had the chance to choose how or

why

I'd choose not to deny the feelings that arise----

　　　When I stop time

HANDS

Hands shaking now, it's just another day –she told herself. Time to rise again, it's time to try; wake up those green eyes to the emptiness of the walls that constrain her very being. She tried though today to not let the dark eyes set in, to not allow the leeches to take the good parts of the mornings light. Such potential she has that one- so many places she is supposed to go and be and see. Tests must be taken that shape her future, still unsure of whether she can do it all on her own... so she sleeps and she dreams. And when she wakes she does not realize the extremity of her dreams or how to decipher the two, how to distinguish the fantasy that in those instances seems so incredibly real.

Life has ways of testing her... of testing all of humanity.

Does she allow her challenges to get the best of her?

Does she find a way to rise?

Does she continue to push in the instances that gratify the dignities of time?

Hollow she feels today. Missing pieces to puzzles that take shape again...

Extreme she is sometimes. Fear she is still unsure of caring much for or about-as its measures seek to succumb her pages. But she wakes up to the light day by day.

Instances–– filled with gratifications of joy

Times where the days seem light, she smiles inside.

Even

Still

She remembers how to love again.

She remembers the fibers engrained in her very being- the kind that cannot be depleted, nor replicated, nor stolen over time

For her gifts are parts of so many souls aching throughout time

As she relates and equates with the people of this place

Understands their pain-mercifully intact

Passed on and on and on- when the masses have forgotten how to give

She gives anyway

Knowing that what matters is truth

Knowing that what matters is inner happiness

A sanctified place where only she can go

           – And only she can have – only she can choose to share

When it is time

Yet still she loves anyway – long and hard and passionately

With every breath and every motion

She moves like the oceans that fill up souls

Shifting pivots unto convoys now

Sails set

Dreaming while waking

- speaking while sleeping

-encompassing the visionaries eyes

Heart sweet and gentle

Body tired but regenerated with each chosen mindset that correlates all of the patterns

All of the messages

All of the missed

All of the watched – all of the angels entity... sometimes all she does is waits for sense to be made

Inspired by what she sees...by what is shown

Deterred from choosing only one dream – she wants to live them all – then remembers graciously that

She already does...

Unity of creativity is upon her mind's eye

For all of us have gifts to share – and lands to shake with light

Beaming – plowing- filling- pouring into every crack and crevasse known

So that reflections may be had and shared

Hands shaking, just another day- shake off the rattling of walking through invisible doorways

-That only she can see – for now

-Time to rise again-AWAKENING- more than she may realize...

Wake up those green eyes

Don't let the dark eyes set in this time

Many places already traveled too, many places yet to see...

She does it all – with guides- just as she guides –

And when she wakes... she does not realize the extremity of her dreams

But

It is the fantasy that in those instances which seem so incredibly real are made so, by transferring the dream into a realm that only she can see, then choose to create----

-Interconnected we are- certainty resides in our wisdom of the truths we contain.

Start Walking

All these things I see

       Does it mean they are me?

Does it mean they are inside of me?

       Paths provide dividends

Of past tense

       With a forward stride

I feel so much deep down inside

       The aspects of each dream

Courses hold strong and I remain on this road

       -So long-

Seen that tree three times by now

       Spirits tell me not to dwell

Keep on moving past

       What seems comfortably noticed

Stay strong

       Hearts wander

But always remain true

       So life

         These places

Seeing the wind

       I desire strongly

To be beside it

    My back confines it, my soul resides in it

But my mind divides it

Into equations of 2 – then 3

    I shift

Should I go—should I be

    I think that getting lost right now is a good answer for me

To sort through

The questions of this task

    Here on Earth

Here on this path

So wise this mind of 20 years past

    Yet so confused

    Because it chooses

    To hold on

To that being that makes her disappear

    Into realms of   sacrifice

Why I do not know

She sees the purity gives an inch   and flies away

Hoping to come

    Back one day

I hope this is real

All that I feel

Conceal

Reminders surround this material place

What is it I have to replace?

What is it that makes me comfortable -in this space?

Nothing -nothing but me

Only me-

She wasn't kidding when she said

Don't ever stop

Never stop

Not for today, not for tomorrow

Never give up

Only flow

Only grow

Only for you

It's your turn this time

The hour grows late and you're conscious

Irritates the flame that itches so bad it burns

I say it's your turn

Clean walls and sparkling walls prove nothing to me- anymore

I want to get dirty

Toil my hands

Explore the world's treasures

    -only

Returning for food or sleep

    I want to take my magical journey of peace of mind

I know where it is

I know what I must find

Too simple

    Give birth

To the idea

Of my name

    So many things does it contain

And my heart

My heart

    Is pure

And I know where it is and where it's been ~

    -dreams convey its beautiful thirst

        And I know

    I know

What my soul has seen

    So deep into the

Forests it's been

        To places only few have seen

Cause only the few can find their way through the mists of autumn

Glowing

Or the sand of undivided time

The pyramids of truth

The dances of a spirit

The paintings of a woman's hand with clay

To meet the one of desire

And the threads of peace conceived in stitches of tangles upon a head so strong

Or the grace of a priestess full of white light and healing advice

All these places I have been

And seen

Old and ancient my water where means of civilizations

Its ability

To create

-something beyond

-what exists now

-here

-before my very eyes

I think the journey I'm about to take

Will make my heart

Feel at home

And my soul feels

Right again

I believe the stars will guide me

Fortunately

I will be

I am already

All I have to do is stop knowing

And start walking

Questioning Oneself

When I am gone will they remember my name?

Will my footsteps be etched into the courses of their veins?

Will my efforts be put into the forefronts of time?

Will my ink strips on pages defining my rhymes be kept inside the worlds of minds?

Will all that I do- matter to most...?

Will my fantasies create dream networks that cast lines to boats?

Will any of it all come to pass... where the state of the dreamer

Has definition and knowledge to grasp?

Will all of my visions remain true to be seen?

Do my photographs of beauty captured in space

      -show the depths of my soul to the rest of this place?

Will everything I love – love me back the same?

Will I ever be able to cease absorbing others pain?

I look into their eyes and I see everything – they talk to me sometimes

And

I can feel it all

A blessing and a curse encompasses its truth

Energies leak disease upon my heart

Shielding their cries

Still – breaths silence – shifting

Yet

In

Still

A vessel I remain, with compassion to heal so long as I maintain

A steady course – like passion to the sun

Have no desire to get back to being numb . . .

So I push past the questions and the thoughts and the pain

The hurt and the anguish

The suffering

The strain

Body aching – the bones seem to touch –

Cause some days all this work has got my body feeling stuck

Giving up – is not my nature

Doesn't work for me

Taught to work towards my dreams

Determination, will, focus, ethics, compassion, morality

Empathy

Love

Stillness quakes

Heart aching for what is drawn I must create

Chest clenching pounding inside some days

Moving

Push on, restore,

Reset and resend – the light encompassing

Her truths concepts

Knowing what is next

Requires just a little bit more. . .

                    For my soul to soar

I move then shift

Angelic wing tipped drifts

When I am gone will they remember my name?

        Will my footsteps be etched into the courses of their veins?

Will my efforts be put into the forefronts of time?

        Will my ink strips on pages defining my rhymes be read and left in the worlds of minds?

Will all that I do matter to most...

Will my fantasies create dream networks that cast lines to boats?

Will any of it all come to pass- where the state of the dreamer has definition and knowledge to grasp?

Will all of my visions remain true to be seen?

The answers remain inside the pages in between

So I write

Dripped ink strips of truth

    Inside the dreams of a dreamer's dream

    One who seeks the harmony of what makes it all complete

    Creating patterns linked symbolically

    Etchings carved into stones

    Repeated in nature

    Found in the grooves

    Of its essence

    The nautilus of a shell

    The triangles overlapping

    Constituting meaning beyond a feeling

    Hold release intertwine when ready

    Carried over and over suspended

    Knowing

    But a fraction of the journey one may seek

    Whose end does not end at all

    Simply moves through it

    Beside it

    Inside it

    Next to it- parallels streaming realigned there is no time here

Its existence is but a mere notion of cages

Affecting networks

And the messages transpired are known somewhere

Someplace deeper then the constructs of one's mind

Its simplicity guides a knowledge not found in books

Its stories told in ancient tongues

Shared inside a child's eyes

An old woman's wisdom shown

A shaman's shifts

A plants sequence

A stars luminescence

None of it fades

For her soul cannot forget where it's been

Her name this time matters not

Only what she does holds' sway

Given – giving – she remains

Tiresome its path but...what is shown....

Is worth of every millisecond of joy encompassing the pain

Its experience yields the reasons

Journeys ties lye inside of life

Life given gives life its meaning

Answering once living the depths of one's name

Footprints etched into the courses of their veins

Efforts put into the forefronts of time

My ink strips on pages defining rhythms

Imprinted into the worlds of minds

For her truths passion

Glows

Through lava tipped streaks

Remember

To Believe

The art of every story moves and creates dream networks that cast lines into the sea

For the vision resides in many forms and many ways

Where the state of the dreamers dream defines the rhythms read

Inside the depths of my heart I remain – it is within oneself that matters most-

That is what creates the paths that kiss the ocean to the sky

That is exactly

HOW HER SOUL WILL CONTINUE TO LOVE ALL SHE SEES
AND LET'S GO of

Flowing now

True inside

The meaning transcribed-

Light beams healing them

CASCADING

POURING

The water that smooth's the stone and all it creates

Waves

Touch changing

Energy flows easy

INTO AND OUT OF THOSE WHO POSSESS

A light beyond the questions we ask

The power that lies inside ones entity

An artist's fine mind holding

Feeling

Everything

As her souls poetry plants seeds

Releasing the passion ties living

Inside — the meaning of my name

11 TIMES OF BEAUTY

11 times of beauty

Passing through a doorway

-blissful peace heavens destinies

Rising now

-coinciding with a

Direction of truth proceeding into levels of unknown travels

But knowing

No questions to wander about in

Simply freedom to seek

Our dreams

Without complication

Only situations that lead into our completion

My soul – I gave

You a piece when

You decided to try

I gave you a piece when you steeped inside

My eyes – so deep

Full of things you have yet to seek

Knowledge, wisdom, freedom, love

A true love – one love –

My love

I believe truly I have found you

And desire to remain forever attached

By links of a chain that are invisible to most

But clear in the

Minds that can see

The point of the vortex I believe we have reached

Euphoric

Causes

Bring new ends

That lye close to the touch

Your touch

-pure poetry

I awaken now----ready now----to understand

Step into – the present moment

Knowing that I have found

The missing link to my heart's demands... at least for a time

Breathing into to it

Fading inside of it

Letting go of it – to click inside----internally match and switch the motions

Hoping

Faith

I now ask myself what is to come next

If ever I am in control of my fate here on this earth

On this treasured palace of moments clung onto and released out of

The soul

Beauty held in our memory bank so sweetly

With hopes and pleasures and imaginations of more

An inkling of understanding past the confusing times where we must ask questions

Sometimes to afraid to answer

Sometimes not

But yet they remain

A part of our minds

And what of the mind

Is it a place that can corrupt the soul if we so let it?

Is it a place that wrinkles the ways of the heart with defeat before we ever try to move past it's never ending mazes and obstacles of time?

Is our purpose always clear?

And how dear Lord... can we make it so?

Constantly reminding ourselves that all shall be what it shall be

And all we need do is trust and love and live our lives eloquently

So softly spoken at times

So roughly crude at others

And here in the whirl winds of life

Similar to that of the tumble cycle that the waves of the great oceans possess

We tumble and tumble and tumble – again and again

That even in the simplest of times it is hard to keep our feet

Or to hold our heads above the rising seas that mean to suck the breath from our lungs

With ease

But to struggle- to fight- to paddle and swim and kick harder and harder

To survive

That is but one of the feats of living

And when completed has a sense of peace

Has a sense of reassurance and truth

Binding us to the trinity that separates us

Asking only- asking – praying oh yes praying

For reassurance that the load we carry will not always feel so very heavy

And our minds can rest

While our eyes see clear

And we begin to trust again

We begin to again believe

In love

A different kind of love that only letting go can maintain

That only the real ones possess

And as it all changes

So does the water, and the river, and the temperatures outside

The wind and the rain set in again

With the memory of warm fires on our toes and colors that feel fuzzy

So she smiles remembering the children

She smiles remembering the purpose

Which holds more reason – more importance and more duty

Than the small troubles of her soul

That at times can diminish clarity or inner ease

Because sometimes what you choose to do in your life is above you

Is more important than you

It is a service to the lost souls of this planet

Who only needed to hear your words

Only need to feel your touch – only need your smile

And some days – just some days you wake up and are blessed enough to

Receive such smiles – such words- such faith

And maybe that is all we really need to hold onto

-Faith

Maybe that's all we need to remember or believe in

That no matter what the question

No matter what the cause, or road, perhaps all we

Truly need is a hope, a divine hope, a divine eye, a divine demeanor

That guides us, that holds us up strong, that gives us back the love we desire so deeply
throughout our lives- the real kind – the right kind

That does not hurt and does not intentionally cause pain or suffering

Only gentle tides of glares between stares under star ridden skies

Sandy toes

And waves of breath that are soothing

Calming to the beat that binds you to something more than a physical reality or space

But a place that no one else can get to

No one else can touch

No one else can see or try to understand

Because only you know where it is

And how to get there

And yet it is no secret – this place- this feeling- this space

Because it belongs to you and no one else

And sometimes you may lose your way

Sometimes the trees may hide the path that you took before

But you still find your way home

You always find your way back to what you care deeply for or about

And although nothing is ever what it seems to be

Sometimes you must trust and believe what your stomach tells you the truth

And what your heart can find

And not be afraid – or have doubt of is beautiful

Because the truth is ---- our faith does not falter, nor fall...

We don't know what is going to happen next, in a moment, in a breath...an hour

In the very next month, or within each year to come

Yet, you can know what is present

What resides in the depths of right now

You can know what you choose

You can know your passions in this life

And I believe that will and does always----bring about the sun

Illuminating rays of light into your life

Cascading light into the lives of those you come across

So enjoy them, those milliseconds of joy- the moments in life that create memories forever in the frameworks of your mind's eye

Rather than waste time wondering how it will work out

Choose to reside in the space of truth

Whose faith proves its resilience time and time again

Humility, faith, gratitude, abundance...

In its roots stems so much growth

Faith my child...you'll see- the lessons transpired soulfully – painfully- beautifully- melodically- inspired by one another's stories

One another's gifts- each uniquely

Communicating

Connecting

Living

Understanding

Compassion-truth-love-loss-light-dark-fought-silence-still-sight-flight

-Encumbered eloquence- giving

Seeing past formality-no judges

Only

-Angelic eyes

Wide-

Receiving

Beyond perception of physical statures and midst's

A person inside the molds melded

Their heart   transpires their meaning

Guiding one another ~ now ~ by caring enough to do so ~ then learning why ~

We all have something to learn and give to every single life.

Guides

I feel as the Native once did

In the valley of time and timelessness

To sit amongst the trees and rejoice in the fields of peace

Long grass grown beside each leg

A pipe stems from his mouth so wide

Wrinkled from the sun

Yet still as young as the skies morning bliss

Amongst a first clouds descent

He soars among a plexus

Of unspoken serenity

------------------A wisdom that grows from trees

So wide

As meadows stream

He takes a sip of the air and all it contains

To purify a spirit inside the backgrounds of glory

Two feathers assemble their way up toward the heavens

Like steaks in the ground

They stand

As straight

As arrows

On top a mountainous peak

        -eyes fixed on a horizon that only he can see

His hands are rough

They have worked for what they've seen

Hair as long as the man ----practically

Parted – equally on each side

To secure the constant reminder

        Of balance

          That he sees

        And knows

        And becomes

        More and more of each passing day

The sun rises and sets

Accepts

Let's go of

Is reminded about

Foresees – encapsulates

Gives a piece too

It is a wondrous

The things people have seen – heard- believe

No worry about one's mind now

No matter where anyone has been or traveled too

Or what it is they see

They accept it

Knowing its connection

As part of the path

Their path

Their truth

Residing frequently as a part of their soul----which guides the heart----protects the body----and pours into every piece of life.

Become What You Create

Things roll over

Change and repeat

Ties bring ends

And windows yield sight

Crossing over

Parallel fields both resuming sexual appeals of yearning

Fading erupting

-inside until there is only questions left

-questions of how or when and sometimes why

Beauty propels through the sky

And divisions partake on a mission of life, of love, of becoming -completed

Just one more step

Just one more try

Just simple peace found inside

Knowing that what the next step may be

Knowing inside what the next step contains

-like the pain or the shattered dream or happiness or

Tranquility

It's all just the same and throughout this journey we proceed

Carry out strategic plans of what to be with

Inside wet coats of melodic bliss

I swish and sway and kiss the cheek of those fading away with

Joy and laughter and reverie

Just when I thought it was gone it would come back to me

Just when I thought it was gone it came back to me

With a single motion – a single decision

The beat maintained a groove and the words came flowing

Overwhelmingly absorbing- into my life, my love, this eloquent unity

Respectfully given

In retrospect I see many things in many colors and many ways

For shadows dreams and expect to find a maze in turn to complicate the way

Then get lost and come back in

Then get lost and release that grin

Of sorrow or relief or shadows of moments in between

Devices unseen to the naked eye

Unseen or even touched by –angels are floating now becoming totally free

-not concerned with what or who or how I should be

Only excited because I made it

I passed the point

I breezed by the fire

I hit the zone passively – peacefully peering into

A paper of sunsets and dreams —–a paper filled with branches and journeys

A picture developed by a visions quest -an inspiration to a child's lonely kiss

Just one look -just one jump-just one single long glare

And I realized I was in heaven

- That miracles do happen on Earthly plains

And that is why we are given life

To see the pink and blue and yellow and orange and violet sunsets

To put our fingers through the sand

To reach out and feel the chill of waves against my hand

To be able to feel the wind at my back blowing my locks from their place -

Purely euphoric

To look at something and walk away with a smile

To walk away from something and realize _everything_

Matters after all

To put on the music and go far away

To listen to the beat and lose control

To leap inside and find only love for everything you do

Because inside you know you gave every piece of you

And that is why

It matters

And now as you close your eyes -you relax

And know - you begin to realize

Purity

Written inside the pages

Of your poetry

Because I became

<u>W</u>hat

I

<u>created</u>

As we evolve as artists and authors, we produce works varying in its complexity and meaning. Many of the pieces in this current work were written from 1995- 2010. I wanted to share a new poem to give my audience an idea of what's yet to come!

Here is a peak of "Living ... & Pure Poetry Volume II."

ORB GUIDES

Perhaps one day the ripples will cease not

But follow

The frequency of photo's streaming

Resurfacing

Microscopic realms of energy

Inhibiting not

But formulating at will

The thought collective

Of

What blue white ORBS FEEL

Like love

Its crossings felt

As she stares at sunrises

And watches birds soar

Above

Everything

Catching glimpses of what

Their souls see...

Memorizing pauses

Their view

Changes ~ ~ ~ the frequency of things

Guiding

Protecting

Calming

Hover pulses

Inside the lights sectors vortex

Staring at the graces inside it

You came to me

Synching once upon a time memories

Guiding me

Mintaka waters sources

Ancient star frequencies

Crystal blue green waters entity

Seas waves ridden

Releasing blocks

Empaths formulation

Walking away

Brain waves scanned syncopated gently

Pulled back in

To your sight

Eyes locked on your center

Shades of cobalt blues

Contrasting the oceans colors movement

Pushing electrodes of love

From your core

Took not the shape of human form

For

I knew you were not of this place

But universes older from the stars

Observing the peace streaming

Energy waves vibrations

Were directly woven through my cells

Frozen portals time laps slips

Recollections flowed

From home

Where it existed

Planet of water and 3 suns in the sky

Where in no negativity dwelled

Cause its existence was never a thought

Corrupting, no...

Only water and light

The white radiating around your blue portal

Brave you were to show yourself to me

Trusting energy

Veins inside white strains

Surrounded by pulses

Multiple waves of directions

As the ocean around you

I could see through your light

But to the right of your gleaming

Were vibrations streaming of another kind

With a hole tunneling through empty space

Almost like if you had to escape or get to another galaxy

That was your gateway

Angelic modes

Beautiful

Penetrable instances

Thank you

For finding me

Your belief revealing truths to me

Found me in the waves

Ridden seas

Sight directions

Pulling me

Clarity

Knowing- seeking- learning

The knowledge cast

Energies stash

No longer masked

But led

Inside lineage

Not of this place

You

Took

Me

Home

Mintaka

Answers revealed

When she chose to acknowledge the questioned

Now pouring

Comfort in

This wisdom

Every bit of her soul's feelings

Justified

Messages transcribed telepathically

The visions stacking

My yearning to go home

To the ocean

But this ocean

Exists in the dusted particles

Star dusted exploded

Cascaded around belts of Orion

Aligning with Alnitak and Alnilam

To the north lies Bellatrix

Pleiades just to the east

Closed my eyes

Realizing the depths of a back burned yearning

To go back home

To a place that no longer exists

But exist it did

And some souls although misplaced

Escaped with their lights purpose

Noticing to let go and build

Once again

For protecting its essence

The sacred

Forms of all

Life's living

Lastly, for now...

My only wish to you all who have shared in this text which stems from my heart is for all of you to live a life filled with love, positivity, and fulfillment. When you decide to choose to do so and then live it- what a movement is created. Its energy comes distinctly from you- and you know it – you can feel it- because you decided to embrace it. With smiles forever lasting and connections relating to precisely what the entity of your souls contain.

It is beautiful- the journey- all of its moments of living- falling- breaking- then deciding to become what you create. Beginning with a vision- stemming from your imagination...then experiencing all of what you do for yourself to make it all become a reality- uniquely – challenging. Once forged, then completed... but always continuing to grow if it's within you. It is freedom. It is profound.

It is my deepest hope that what I have written and chosen to share with the world brings the world light, love, and understanding- insight unto oneself – for these pages have been designed from the depths of my passions, from the depths of my journey thus far. It never ends and it always begins...so may you always continue to find exactly what your heart craves- then go for it- even if it takes a lifetime- it doesn't matter. All that matters is that you chose to do what you love- and this time I can say I am glad that I chose to give this fraction of the pieces I have designed. Volume II of "Living... & Pure Poetry" is on its way soon.

In the meantime, may we rise as our dimensions expand for humanity is love. And human beings are operating on frequencies that for once I am happy to say they are accepting. May we continue this streaming of positivity, truth, love and light.

Imagery & Poetry
Jamie Cowling
The Art of Every Story

Instagram imagery.poetryjlc
Poetry: https://soundcloud.com/lovelife2020
Email: imagery.poetry.jlc@gmail.com

Jamie Cowling, a native to the shorelines of Asbury Park, N.J. is a soul full of energy, love, and artistry. Author, poet, surfer, songstress, visual artist and educator- this woman works not only for her career as a teacher, but for every creative passion she has inside.

The medium matters not to Jamie- so long as it flows. A writer since childhood, she paid attention to waves of things. Her truths influenced by the art of every story searching for "the heartbeat."

Someone once asked me why I write...what inspires me?

I said...

"I write what I feel and I feel a great many things all the time. And when I am lucky enough to transcribe the pieces- their energy- it comes from a place sacred to me. Inside the images visions that stream from the depths of one-self.

Fast or slow-it all has a rhythm...   but sometimes...

The horizon smiles back reflecting the dreamscapes....   and it is in these milliseconds therein lain the links, captivating- capturing- and embracing what is felt.

It is the wave swells energy- the layers connecting the grooves.

    In these moments ...   I let go...

       In these moments I become... ~~~ the heartbeat."   ~~~~

~~~ Jamie continues to work to preserve the arts in local communities, especially amongst the youth. With the help of many she continues to collaborate with artists to create spaces for young people to be exposed to the arts and form their own kinds of expression. This vision is and has been a collective/village effort and continues to grow. Gratitude and respect she sends to "her tribe" that work selflessly to keep the pathways open. ~~~